CLASSICAL RECORDINGS

CLASSIC *f*M
HANDY
GUIDES

CLASSICAL RECORDINGS

SAM JACKSON

First published 2015 by
Elliott and Thompson Limited
27 John Street
London WC1N 2BX
www.eandtbooks.com

ISBN: 978-1-78396-056-9

Text © Classic FM 2015

9 8 7 6 5 4 3 2 1

A catalogue record for this book is available from the
British Library.

Typesetting: Marie Doherty
Printed in the UK by TJ International Ltd

Contents

Introduction

At Classic FM, we spend a lot of our time dreaming up wonderful ways of making sure that as many people as possible across the UK have the opportunity to listen to classical music. As the nation's biggest classical music radio station, we feel that we have a responsibility to share the world's greatest music as widely as we can.

Over the years, we have written a variety of classical music books in all sorts of shapes and sizes. But we have never put together a series of books quite like this.

This set of books covers a whole range of aspects of classical music. They are all written in Classic FM's friendly, accessible style and you can rest assured that they are packed full of facts about classical music. Read separately, each book gives you a handy snapshot of a particular subject area. Added together, the series combines to offer a more detailed insight into the full story of classical music. Along the way, we shall be paying particular attention to some of the key composers whose music we play most often on the radio station, as well as examining many of classical music's subgenres.

These books are relatively small in size, so they are not going to be encyclopedic in their level of detail; there are other books out there that do that much better than we could ever hope to. Instead, they are intended to be enjoyable introductory guides that will be particularly useful to listeners who are beginning their voyage of discovery through the rich and exciting world of classical music. Drawing on the research we have undertaken for many of our previous Classic FM books, they concentrate on information rather than theory because we want to make this series of books attractive and inviting to readers who are not necessarily familiar with the more complex aspects of musicology.

For more information on this series, take a look at our website: www.ClassicFM.com/handyguides.

Preface

In the world of pop and rock, buying music is a fairly simple affair. Let's say you're a fan of Katy Perry or Arctic Monkeys: you simply download the songs you love, or purchase a copy of their latest CD. The world of classical music, however, tends to be a more complicated affair. Imagine you've just heard Vaughan Williams' *The Lark Ascending* for the very first time, and you want to get your hands on a copy. A quick search online will present you with enough CDs to fill your entire living room. Do you go for Nigel Kennedy's long, languid version? Or Sarah Chang's speedier (but arguably no less beautiful) performance? And then there's Tasmin Little, Janine Jansen and Julia Fischer to consider – not to mention the fact that some of the recordings seem quite pricey, while others are cheaper than a cappuccino. In short: when it comes to buying classical music, where on earth do you start – and how, exactly, do you discern what's 'good' or 'bad'?

This new pocket guide from Classic FM aims to set you on the right path towards building up a great classical music collection, whether that's in the form of physical CDs or a multitude of downloads. Over the next few pages, you'll discover which classical record labels are worth your attention, before we then dive head first into the 100 Albums to Own. Based on *The Classic FM Hall of Fame* (also available from Elliott & Thompson), it focuses on the most popular classical repertoire and, each time, includes a suggestion of a great recording for you to purchase.

It goes without saying that any list like this is, by its very nature, subjective. You only have to read the critics to quickly see that one person's definition of success can sometimes be another person's turkey. But whether or not you agree with the choices, they should hopefully give you a starting point when it comes to what you should be spending your money on.

If you want to find out more about the best classical recordings, do join David Mellor every

Saturday evening at 9 p.m. on Classic FM, for *The New Releases Show*. Every week, David picks a Best Bargain, a Young Artist to Watch, a Connoisseurs' Choice and an Album of the Week, playing music from a wide range of the latest releases. What's more, you'll find pages of resources and suggestions on our website, ClassicFM.com – just click on 'Discover' at the top of the home page, and within a matter of moments you'll be exploring a wealth of expert opinion.

Happy listening!

The Classical Labels
That Matter

There are hundreds of classical record labels – and it's certainly the case that 'big' doesn't always mean 'best'. Having said that, if you're looking for a mark of quality, you can be sure that these very successful labels are nearly always home to recordings you can rely on. So, in alphabetical order, here's a rundown of the classical labels that matter.

Chandos

A family company based in Colchester, Chandos is known for championing esoteric repertoire alongside the more well-known names. The Chandos strapline is 'Serious about Classical Music', so you won't find many jazzy covers, jokey sleeve notes or controversial repertoire here. What you will find, though, is a label that's absolutely committed to a huge range of music, always performed to an extremely high standard.

Decca

The Decca label has had an intriguing and impressive history: as well as being home to the likes of Luciano Pavarotti and Alfred Brendel, it was also the label of choice for Billie Holiday, Louis Armstrong and the Rolling Stones, among others. Today, Decca exists in two distinct forms: Decca Classics (which, with its blue and red label, is home to mainstream classical artists such as the young pianist Benjamin Grosvenor and the conductor Riccardo Chailly) and Decca Records (the black-labelled other half of the company that includes crossover stars such as Katherine Jenkins and Alfie Boe).

Deutsche Grammophon

Deutsche Grammophon – or DG as it's referred to by many – can lay claim to being not just the most important classical music label, but the most important label in the history of all recorded music. Founded in Hanover in 1898, Deutsche Grammophon was responsible for launching the world's first record- and gramophone-manufacturing works. Well over a century later, DG's prestigious yellow label has become shorthand for excellence and quality.

Harmonia Mundi

Harmonia Mundi is the world's oldest independent record label: since 1958, this French company has championed classical music in all its glorious forms. In particular, Harmonia Mundi is known for releasing Baroque music performed on period instruments, of the kind that Bach and Handel would have been familiar with. The label employs around 300 people worldwide; its founder, the much-loved Bernard Coutaz, died in 2010 and was succeeded by his daughter, Eva, who is now president of the company.

Hyperion

The success and appeal of the Hyperion label lies in its quirkiness, its originality, and its discovery of some of the most remarkable repertoire. The founding of the company is fairly idiosyncratic: it was the brainchild of a music-loving taxi driver called Ted Perry, who launched Hyperion in 1980. Perry had worked in record shops as a young man and he saw a gap in the market for enjoyable, well-packaged classical music that was not necessarily well known. Despite its extensive back catalogue and worldwide acclaim, Hyperion remains a family company: Ted's son, Simon, now runs the business from an industrial estate in south-east London.

LSO Live

The London Symphony Orchestra is a world-class ensemble, admired across the globe for its outstanding music making. However, despite the fact that the LSO made their first recording all the way back in 1913, it wasn't until 2000 that they launched their own record label. LSO Live is home to some outstanding recordings: Valery Gergiev's interpretations of Russian music, for example, and Sir Colin Davis's explorations of the music of Nielsen, Sibelius and Haydn. What's more, LSO Live was one of the first classical labels to truly understand the importance of digital downloads, and it remains one of the most innovative and impressive outfits around.

Naxos

The philosophy of Naxos is quite different from that of all the other labels mentioned here: unlike its rivals, the company does not primarily focus on well-known performers. Instead, Naxos is first and foremost a repertoire-driven company, providing recordings for people who often know what music they like but who don't necessarily mind by whom it's performed. What's special about Naxos is the price: in the UK, nearly all the company's classical albums currently sell for £5.99, which is less than half the price you would expect to pay for the same repertoire on many other labels.

Onyx Classics

Onyx is a quirky little label – but none the worse for that. It's not one of 'the majors', with a vast back-room team and a significant marketing spend to boot, but the company consistently puts out recordings of mighty fine quality. Take, for example, their autumn 2014 release of orchestral music by Prokofiev, performed by the Bournemouth Symphony Orchestra under Kirill Karabits: five-star reviews all round, with an album that puts most of its competitors in the shade. Onyx is an imaginative label, creating really interesting releases of a wide variety of repertoire – and their ability to discover new artists also marks them out as a real success story.

Sony Classical

As the label of choice for world-famous soloists such as the Chinese pianist Lang Lang and the American violinist Joshua Bell, Sony Classical is definitely worthy of your attention. When you add the fact that this is the label that champions modern-day film scores more than pretty much all the other major companies combined, Sony Classical is indisputably one of the most important players in all classical music.

Warner Classics

It's only relatively recently that the name Warner Classics has also included the EMI Classics back catalogue. Prior to various corporate changes, Warner Classics specialised in box sets and reissues, taking its back catalogue of impressive recordings from the twentieth century and presenting it to consumers in a new, often cost-effective way. Before the company subsumed EMI Classics and Virgin Classics, it released a wide range of excellent recordings – and now the Warner Classics brand is one of the premium names in classical music.

The 100 Albums
to Own

1 **Sergei Rachmaninov:** *Piano Concerto No. 2*
   Stephen Hough (piano). Dallas Symphony
   Orchestra conducted by Andrew Litton
   Hyperion CDA 675012
   2-CD set, including all four of Rachmaninov's
   piano concertos

As the nation's most popular concerto, it's no surprise that there are hundreds of recordings of Rachmaninov's *Piano Concerto No. 2* – but not all of them would be met with approval by the composer himself. In the case of Stephen Hough, however, Rachmaninov would surely give the great British soloist an enormous pat on the back (his hand span was huge, by the way) for interpreting this mighty work in such a faithful manner. Hough dazzles with his dexterity, and teases out the middle movement's most tender melodies, with outstanding accompaniment from the Dallas Symphony Orchestra under Andrew Litton.

2 Wolfgang Amadeus Mozart: *Clarinet Concerto*
Michael Collins (clarinet). Swedish
Chamber Orchestra
Chandos CHAN 10756
With works by Aaron Copland and
Elena Kats-Chernin

Since the invention of the gramophone, there have been many fine interpretations of Mozart's autumnal *Clarinet Concerto* – but it's a recent recording of the work that gets the Classic FM seal of approval. The British clarinettist Michael Collins won the woodwind round of the Young Musician of the Year competition all the way back in 1978, and he's since gone on to become one of the most in-demand soloists of his generation. Here, he combines the roles of clarinettist and conductor, performing the Mozart concerto alongside the Swedish Chamber Orchestra. He's actually playing a 'basset clarinet' – the original instrument for which the concerto was written – which has a slightly lower register than the standard B flat clarinet.

3   Max Bruch: *Violin Concerto No. 1*
Julia Fischer (violin). Tonhalle Orchestra of Zurich
conducted by David Zinman
Decca Classics 478 3544
With Dvořák's Violin Concerto

The German violinist Julia Fischer is, quite simply, an
outstanding performer – and her recording of Bruch's
perennially popular *Violin Concerto No. 1* is full of
energy and verve. Still only in her early thirties, Fischer
already has a mantelpiece heaving with prestigious
awards, including First Prize at the International
Yehudi Menuhin Competition when she was aged
just twelve and Artist of the Year at the Classic FM
Gramophone Awards in 2007. Here, she joins forces
with the brilliant conductor David Zinman, whose
Tonhalle Orchestra of Zurich is the perfect partner
for Fischer's wonderfully rich, passionate playing. Plus,
if you buy this album, you also get Fischer's take on
the Dvořák *Violin Concerto*: less well known than the
Bruch, certainly, but still definitely worth discovering.

4   Ralph Vaughan Williams: *The Lark Ascending*
Nigel Kennedy (violin). City of Birmingham
Symphony Orchestra conducted by Simon Rattle
Warner Classics 562 8132
With Elgar's Violin Concerto

'He rises and begins to round/He drops the silver

chain of sound/Of many links without a break/In chirrup, whistle, slur and shake.' So begins the George Meredith poem that inspired Vaughan Williams' most famous work, *The Lark Ascending*. There have been many fine recordings of it over the years but the most beautiful of them all is arguably the one by Nigel Kennedy and the City of Birmingham Symphony Orchestra. At just under eighteen minutes in duration, it's a full four minutes longer than some other versions – but the space and depth created by Kennedy and the CBSO, expertly conducted by Simon Rattle, helps to fully convey this gloriously British piece of music.

5   Edward Elgar: *Cello Concerto*
Jamie Walton (cello). Philharmonia Orchestra
conducted by Alexander Briger
Signum SIGCD 116
With Myaskovsky's Cello Concerto

'This is probably the best performance of the Elgar Cello Concerto … [Jamie] Walton cannot be beaten.' So said the Elgar Society, no less, when Walton's recording of this warhorse of British music was released in 2008. For so many people, Jacqueline du Pré's interpretation of the piece is the must-have recording – but this more modern take on it, from another English cellist, is arguably even better. Walton is very ably accompanied by the Philharmonia Orchestra, Classic FM's Orchestra on Tour, conducted by Alexander Briger; even if you know the piece well, prepare to hear it afresh when you experience this five-star performance.

6   Ludwig van Beethoven: *Piano Concerto No. 5 ('Emperor')*

Alfred Brendel (piano). Vienna Philharmonic Orchestra conducted by Simon Rattle
Philips 462 7812
3-CD set including all five of Beethoven's piano concertos

Beethoven's *'Emperor' Piano Concerto* is one of his most famous works, but the composer himself did not give it its nickname. Instead, so the story goes, it derives from a comment made by one of Napoleon's officers, who was stationed in Vienna at the time of the work's premiere. It was 'an emperor of a concerto', the man supposedly exclaimed. Indeed it was; and the name has stuck ever since. When it comes to an emperor of a pianist, look no further than the legendary Alfred Brendel – who, when joined by the Vienna Philharmonic Orchestra under Simon Rattle, brings this concerto vividly and, at times, playfully to life.

7 Ludwig van Beethoven: *Symphony No. 6* ('*Pastoral*')

Budapest Festival Orchestra conducted by
Iván Fischer
Channel Classics CCS SA 30710
With Beethoven's Symphony No. 4

There are many fine boxed sets of Beethoven's complete symphonies: every major orchestra has committed them to disc at some point, often more than once, and if you want a great complete set you can do a lot worse than get hold of the recordings on LSO Live from Bernard Haitink and the London Symphony Orchestra. But if you're after the '*Pastoral*' alone, give the version from the Budapest Festival Orchestra under Iván Fischer a try. Lush strings, perky woodwind and a wonderfully pure brass sound all combine to create a fine musical evocation of the countryside.

8 Edward Elgar: *Variations on an Original Theme* ('*Enigma Variations*')

Hallé Orchestra conducted by Mark Elder
CDHLL 7501

Music doesn't come more English than '*Nimrod*', so it seems only right to pick a recording of Elgar's *Enigma Variations* that hails from these shores. There's a fine historic one from the Royal Philharmonic Orchestra under Yehudi Menuhin (Regis RRC 1219) and a great recording from the London Symphony Orchestra and Colin Davis (LSO Live 0109) – but the one you really shouldn't be without comes from the Manchester-based Hallé Orchestra, conducted by Mark Elder. The strings of the Hallé are particularly vivid here – and, over-all, the sound quality is outstanding. Mark Elder is known for being a peerless conductor of Elgar's music; you'll find ample proof of that here.

9   Ludwig van Beethoven: *Symphony No. 9 ('Choral')*

Luba Orgonasova (soprano), Anne Sofie von Otter (mezzo-soprano), Anthony Rolfe Johnson (tenor), Gilles Cachemaille (bass). The Monteverdi Choir and the Orchestre Révolutionnaire et Romantique conducted by John Eliot Gardiner
DG Archiv 439 9002

As mentioned above, there are many boxed sets of the Beethoven symphonies – and if you like this version of *No. 9*, you might like to know that it's also available as part of a complete symphonies pack-age. This particular recording isn't totally faultless: at times, the speed at which Gardiner takes things is certainly eyebrow-raising. But it's worth getting hold of for the *'Ode to Joy'* alone: simply outstanding singing from the four soloists, combined with the stunning sounds of the Monteverdi Choir, on top form here. A mighty and powerful conclusion to one of the most important symphonies ever composed.

10 Johann Pachelbel: *Canon*
Il Giardino Armonico
Warner Classics 2564 632642
A collection of Baroque masterpieces, including music by Albinoni, Bach, Vivaldi and others, the ninth of an eleven-volume series

It might be hard to believe, given the ubiquity of this particular tune, but Pachelbel's *Canon* didn't actually become well known the world over until the twentieth century, when it was published by a German scholar in an article about the composer's music. Nowadays, whether experienced as on-hold call-centre music or heard in an altogether more joyful setting at a wedding, this simple yet beautiful Baroque composition is one of the most famous pieces of classical music. Some versions are a bit soupy but this one, from the Baroque ensemble Il Giardino Armonico, is bright, bouncy and joyful; exactly as the composer would have intended.

11 Samuel Barber: *Adagio for Strings*

Detroit Symphony Orchestra conducted by
Neeme Järvi
Chandos CHAN 9169
With symphonies by Barber and George Frederick Bristow

Just as it seems logical to choose an English recording
of Elgar's *Enigma Variations*, so it feels right to point
you in the direction of an American version of Samuel
Barber's most famous piece, the *Adagio for Strings*.
The work was written originally for string quartet,
before the composer himself went on to orchestrate it
for a full string ensemble. He had the great conductor
Arturo Toscanini to thank for this: after hearing the
quartet's second movement, Toscanini told Barber he
had a hit on his hands and he urged him to turn it
into a stand-alone piece. Here, the *Adagio for Strings*
is performed by the Detroit Symphony Orchestra,
with Neeme Järvi deftly teasing out the beautiful
melodies and lush harmonies.

12 Edvard Grieg: *Piano Concerto*

Leif Ove Andsnes (piano). Berlin Philharmonic
Orchestra conducted by Mariss Jansons
Warner Classics 0946 3943992
With other piano music by Grieg

How, you wonder, would Grieg feel about the fact
that many of us associate this particular piece of

music with Morecambe and Wise? Eric's version of the piece, conducted by André 'Andrew Preview' Previn, is one of the most memorable TV sketches of all time, frequently coming towards the top of those seemingly endless countdowns to find the nation's favourite funny moment. The concerto itself was no laughing matter for Grieg, though. At the age of twenty-five, the young Norwegian composer was determined to make his mark on the world with this, his first work to employ an orchestra. And in this particular recording, Grieg's fellow Norwegian, the pianist Leif Ove Andsnes, certainly makes *his* mark, with a thrilling performance alongside the Berlin Phil and Mariss Jansons.

13 Camille Saint-Saëns: *Symphony No. 3* (*'Organ Symphony'*)
Michael Matthes (organ). Bastille Opera Orchestra conducted by Myung-Whun Chung
Deutsche Grammophon 435 8542
With Messiaen's L'Ascension

Franz Liszt, no less, once described Camille Saint-Saëns as 'the greatest organist in the world', and it's certainly true that this fine French composer was equally adept at the keyboards and pedals of the organ as he was in front of a piece of manuscript paper. He certainly knew how to write for the instrument, as is borne out by this mighty work. The recording you should definitely invest in comes from a fellow Frenchman, the brilliant organist Michael Matthes. He's joined by the Bastille Opera Orchestra, conducted by Myung-Whun Chung, for a captivating performance of Saint-Saëns' most popular piece of music. Incidentally, we have the Royal Philharmonic Society to thank for commissioning this work: the composer himself conducted the premiere at the old St James's Hall in London, which is now the site of the Le Meridien Hotel in Piccadilly.

14 Ralph Vaughan Williams: *Fantasia on a Theme by Thomas Tallis*

Britten Sinfonia conducted by Nicholas Cleobury
Classic FM CFMCD 44
With works by Delius and Elgar

In 1908, Ralph Vaughan Williams travelled to Paris to study orchestration with Maurice Ravel. It proved to be an inspiring experience: when he returned home, he undertook one of his most fruitful periods of composition. The year 1910 saw the premiere of not just his mighty first symphony (*A Sea Symphony*), but also of the *Fantasia on a Theme by Thomas Tallis*

– at the Three Choirs Festival in Gloucester. In this performance of the work from the string players of the Britten Sinfonia, it's amply clear that Vaughan Williams' focus on orchestration definitely paid off. It's a rich and unmistakably British sound, expertly conveyed by this fine English ensemble.

15 Georges Bizet: *'Au fond du temple saint'* from *The Pearl Fishers*
Jussi Björling (tenor), Robert Merrill (baritone). RCA Victor Symphony Orchestra conducted by Renato Cellini
RCA 447 9133

It's fair to say that the reason for this opera's annual inclusion in the Classic FM Hall of Fame is due not to *The Pearl Fishers* in its eighty-minute entirety, but to one particular duet featuring the tenor and baritone: *'Au fond du temple saint'*. Sung by the characters Zuria and Nadir, caught in a love triangle with the one girl they're both after, the duet has been performed thousands of times in its own right in the concert hall. Jussi Björling and Robert Merrill capture Bizet's music magically in their definitive 1950s recording; other versions worth discovering include the dream partnership of Roberto Alagna and Bryn Terfel.

16 Gustav Holst: *The Planets*

London Philharmonic Orchestra conducted by
Adrian Boult

Warner Classics 627 8982

Holst's *The Planets* is far and away the most famous
work by this twentieth-century English composer.
The popularity of three sections of the suite, in
particular (namely: *Mars*, *Venus* and *Jupiter*) have
helped to make it one of the best-known pieces in
the entire classical repertoire. It comes as no surprise, then, to discover that there are hundreds of
recordings of *The Planets*, many of which have sold
by the bucket-load. And when it comes to the one
version you shouldn't be without, it's this historic
interpretation from the brilliant British conductor Adrian Boult and the London Philharmonic
Orchestra.

17 Antonín Dvořák: *Symphony No. 9 ('From the New World')*

Vienna Philharmonic Orchestra conducted by
István Kertész

Esoteric ESSD 90015

There are many very fine modern recordings of
Dvořák's most famous symphony, and if you're
after one of those, you won't be disappointed with

the version by the Oslo Philharmonic Orchestra conducted by Mariss Jansons. But when it comes to the real must-have performance, attention turns to a remastered version of a 1961 recording, featuring a thirty-two-year-old István Kertész at the helm of the Vienna Philharmonic Orchestra. Taut, thrilling and full of explosive energy, this is the *'New World'* as you've never heard it before. And the gloriously sedate slow movement provides another compelling reason to add this one to your collection.

18 George Frideric Handel: *Messiah*

Kerstin Avemo (soprano), Patricia Bardon
(mezzo-soprano), Lawrence Zazzo (counter-tenor),
Kobie van Rensburg (tenor), Neal Davies
(bass-baritone). Choir of Clare College,
Cambridge, and Freiburg Baroque Orchestra
conducted by René Jacobs
Harmonia Mundi HMC 901928/29
2-CD set

Handel's most popular work, and the world's most famous oratorio, has been recorded by a great many orchestras, choirs and soloists, and there's a clutch of outstanding recordings to choose from. This one, masterminded by the Belgian conductor René Jacobs, is much more stripped back than many others you could purchase; as the name of his ensemble suggests, the Freiburg Baroque Orchestra performs music in a historically faithful style, using instruments and techniques of the Baroque period. The voices of the Choir of Clare College, Cambridge, and a quartet of excellent soloists play a large part in making this a very special recording indeed.

19 Wolfgang Amadeus Mozart: *Requiem*

Barbara Bonney (soprano), Anne Sofie von Otter (mezzo-soprano), Hans Peter Blochwitz (tenor), Willard White (bass). Monteverdi Choir and English Baroque Soloists conducted by John Eliot Gardiner

Philips 420 1972

With another setting of the Kyrie text by Mozart

When it comes to the popularity of Mozart's music, his sublime *Requiem* is second only to the *Clarinet Concerto* in terms of Classic FM listeners' affections. Mozart himself never completed the work: it was finished off by his pupil, Franz Xaver Süssmayr, shortly after the composer's death. Felicity Lott and Willard White are both on particularly fine form in their Warner Classics recording of the *Requiem* with the London Philharmonic Orchestra, but

White pips himself to the post in another version, which sees him perform alongside three other soloists including the soprano Barbara Bonney, plus the English Baroque Soloists and the Monteverdi Choir. The outstanding conductor John Eliot Gardiner is on the podium.

20 Sergei Rachmaninov: *Symphony No. 2*
Orchestra of the National Academy of St Cecilia
conducted by Antonio Pappano
Warner Classics 949 4622
With Lyadov's The Enchanted Lake

The immediacy of the romance in Rachmaninov's music is probably the greatest reason for its widespread and continued appeal. Very few composers manage so instantly to grab the attention of their listeners, transporting them to another place in the space of a few bars of music. And in Rachmaninov's case, nowhere is this better demonstrated than in the third movement of his *Symphony No. 2*. On this particular recording, released in 2011, that movement comes in at just shy of sixteen minutes – substantially longer than on many other versions. And this rich, expansive approach is just one of the things that makes this superb recording so incredibly rewarding.

21 Antonio Vivaldi: *The Four Seasons*

Nigel Kennedy (violin). English
Chamber Orchestra
Warner Classics 2564 628814

In September 2014, Warner Classics marked the twenty-fifth anniversary of the release of one of the biggest classical albums of all time by issuing this special edition of an incredibly successful recording: namely, Nigel Kennedy's version of Vivaldi's *The Four Seasons*. There are other interpretations of this ubiquitous piece that one could argue are 'better', but it would seem churlish not to recommend such a phenomenally successful, record-breaking release. To quote Kennedy himself: 'My first recording of *The Four Seasons* was the first really popular classical album, even if I say it myself, before Pavarotti and before Vanessa Mae and before any of the mo-fos who made the big waves in classical music.'

22 Mascagni: *Cavalleria rusticana*

Julia Varady (soprano), Piero Cappuccilli
(baritone), Luciano Pavarotti (tenor). London
Opera Chorus and National Philharmonic
Orchestra conducted by Gianandrea Gavezzeni
Decca E444 3912

As is the case with a number of operatic entries in the Classic FM Hall of Fame, the inclusion of

Mascagni's *Cavalleria rusticana* primarily comes down to one section: in this case, the beautiful 'Intermezzo'. But the chosen recording here is of the complete opera, which really is well worth discovering in its entirety. It features a relatively young Luciano Pavarotti, joining forces with two other soloists to perform in an opera that Mascagni wrote when he was just twenty-seven years old. If only he could have composed a successful follow-up, he might not have died almost penniless in liberated Italy in 1945.

23 Gregorio Allegri: *Miserere*

Choir of New College, Oxford, conducted by Edward Higginbottom
Erato 3984 295882
2-CD set of choral music from the Baroque to the present day

Allegri's *Miserere* is a sublime nine-voice setting of Psalm 51: 'Miserere mei, Deus, secundum magnam misercodiam tuam' ('Have mercy upon me, O God, after Thy great goodness'). As you listen to the heavenly sound of each interweaving voice in the Choir of New College, Oxford, it's interesting to note that Allegri actually composed the piece for two separate choirs: one of four voices, and the other of five. The peerless singing of this world-class choir commutes the very deep spirituality in Allegri's music; as is so often the case, they are expertly led by the College's Director of Music, Edward Higginbottom.

24 Joaquín Rodrigo: *Concierto de Aranjuez*
Julian Bream (guitar). City of Birmingham
Symphony Orchestra conducted
by Simon Rattle
Warner Classics CDC 754 6612
With guitar works by Malcolm Arnold and
Toru Takemitsu

When it comes to recordings, this summery guitar concerto has had an interesting history. Miles Davis was inspired by the *Concierto de Aranjuez*, adapting it for his 1960 album *Sketches of Spain*, and it was put to famously good use in the 1996 film *Brassed Off!*, which saw miners affectionately referring to it as 'Orange Juice' due to the difficulties of pronouncing 'Aranjuez'. Fun as both those versions might be, it's this one from the legendary British guitarist Julian Bream that definitely ticks all the boxes. Wonderfully precise playing, and sensitive and warm accompaniment from the City of Birmingham Symphony Orchestra, all under the expert eye of Simon Rattle.

25 Gabriel Fauré: *Requiem*
Grace Davidson (soprano). Tenebrae and
London Symphony Orchestra Chamber Ensemble
conducted by Nigel Short
LSO Live LSO 0728
With Bach's Violin Partita No. 2 and a selection of chorales

In this seven-section requiem, the French composer
distilled some of the most beautiful melodies he
ever composed. The creation was almost certainly
a musical tribute to his father, who died in 1885,
three years before work on the piece began. And
in this relatively recent recording from the choir
Tenebrae and the LSO Chamber Ensemble, the
poignancy and beauty of this reflective masterpiece
are very powerfully rendered. The performance is
directed by Nigel Short; his wife, the soprano Grace
Davidson, is the soprano in the *'Pie Jesu'*. Give it a
listen and you'll find it hard to disagree with the
suggestion that she truly has a voice from heaven.

26 Jean Sibelius: *Finlandia*
Bergen Philharmonic Orchestra conducted by
Andrew Davis
Chandos CHSA 5134
*With orchestral music by Sibelius, including his
Violin Concerto*

There are stacks of fine recordings of *Finlandia*

– for starters, everyone should give Herbert von Karajan's interpretation with the Berlin Phil a listen at some point. But this recent version, issued in 2014, is a real corker, too. Andrew Davis is one of those conductors who doesn't seem to attract the star treatment; he's not a big name in the sense of a Gergiev, or a Dudamel, or a Rattle. But he's one of this country's finest maestros, as demonstrated here in this fulsome, expansive recording of one of the world's best nationalistic works. What's more, if you buy the full album, you'll also get a great version of the Sibelius *Violin Concerto* featuring former Young Musician of the Year winner, Jennifer Pike.

27 Felix Mendelssohn: *Violin Concerto*

James Ehnes (violin). Philharmonia Orchestra
conducted by Vladimir Ashkenazy
Onyx 4060
With Mendelssohn's Octet

Anyone aspiring to be a concert violinist simply has to have this one in his or her repertoire. Nearly 150 years after its composition, Mendelssohn's *Violin Concerto* remains one of the most regularly performed and most loved of all instrumental concertos. The work was one of the first to be recorded by the star Scottish violinist Nicola Benedetti – something of which the teenage Mendelssohn, who was inspired to compose this piece at a young age, would surely approve – but it's the recording by the Canadian violinist James Ehnes that you shouldn't be without. Beautiful phrasing, richly played melodies both high and low, and impressively speedy passages in the outer movements all combine to make this a must-have.

28 Wolfgang Amadeus Mozart: *Piano Concerto No. 21 ('Elvira Madigan')*
Murray Perahia (piano). English
Chamber Orchestra
Sony Essential Classics 34562 (reissue)
With Mozart's Piano Concerto No. 9

This is another work that has been interpreted in wildly different ways over the years. Take the famous second movement: Daniel Barenboim performs it at a slow, sedate pace, taking over eight minutes from start to finish. The young Norwegian pianist Christian Ilhe Hadland, meanwhile, has everything done and dusted in under six minutes. As always, to get a feel for what you enjoy the most, the key is to listen to as many versions as possible but, as a first step, you definitely won't be disappointed with Murray Perahia's graceful recording of Mozart's most popular piano concerto. He plays the dual role of pianist and conductor here, leading the English Chamber Orchestra from the keyboard.

29 Gustav Mahler: *Symphony No. 5*
San Francisco Symphony Orchestra
conducted by Michael Tilson Thomas
San Francisco Symphony 821936 00122

The celebrated American conductor Michael Tilson Thomas celebrated his seventieth birthday in December 2014, and over the last few decades he's received a stream of five-star reviews for his recordings. This one, with the San Francisco Symphony Orchestra, is a marvellous rendition of Mahler's most famous symphony, introduced to millions for the first time when its fourth movement 'Adagietto' was used in Luchino Visconti's 1971 film *Death in Venice*. Mahler is famous for the way in which he stretched classical music to its limits; and yet, despite all the grandness of scale and depth in his works, the enduring popularity of the *Symphony No. 5* is due to one of the quietest, most tender movements ever composed.

30 Ludwig van Beethoven:

Symphony No. 7
Scottish Chamber Orchestra
conducted by Charles Mackerras
Hyperion CDS 44304
With Beethoven's Symphony No. 8, in a 5-CD set of
Beethoven's complete symphonies

Described by Richard Wagner, no less, as 'the apoth-
eosis of the dance', this four-movement symphony
begins in grave, sombre tones. Not for Beethoven
to refer back to the stirring opening to the Fifth,
or the lilting, sunny start to the Sixth; instead, the
orchestral colours are dark, creating a sense of fore-
boding about what's to come. The Scottish Chamber
Orchestra under Charles Mackerras captures this
brilliantly, and the ensemble manages to convey
simultaneously the lightness of touch in later parts
of the symphony. The unbounded finale, meanwhile, was apparently summed up by Tchaikovsky
as 'a whole series of images, full of unrestrained joy,
full of bliss and pleasure of life'. Nowhere is that
more evident than in this recording.

31 Sergei Rachmaninov: *Rhapsody on a Theme of Paganini*

Nikolai Lugansky (piano). City of
Birmingham Symphony Orchestra
conducted by Sakari Oramo
Warner Classics 2564 636752
3-CD set including all Rachmaninov's piano concertos

This piano-concerto-like work was the 1934 equivalent of sampling a pop song. Had he lived to hear it, the nineteenth-century Italian composer Niccolò Paganini would surely have been flattered to discover that Rachmaninov, of all people, had chosen his *Caprice No. 24* for solo violin as the inspiration for an ingenious theme and variations for piano and orchestra. And both Paganini and Rachmaninov would surely approve of this dazzling recording from Nikolai Lugansky and the CBSO, which manages to dazzle and tug at the heart strings in equal measure. There's great ensemble between soloist and orchestra here, but if you want to know what Rachmaninov thinks the piece should definitively sound like, you can still buy his own recording of it, too.

32 Johann Sebastian Bach: *Double Violin Concerto*

Rachel Podger (violin), Bojan Čičič (violin).

Brecon Baroque

Channel Classics CCSSA 34113

With Bach's other double and triple concertos

When it comes to Baroque music, a great deal of which was composed by Johann Sebastian Bach, there are huge variations in how musicians and critics view what's known as 'period performance'; in other words, whether it's right for Baroque works to be played on modern instruments, or on instruments made within the composer's own lifetime. If you want to hear Bach as Bach himself would have heard it, this recording is a very good place to start. Crisp, clear and elegant, it has all the natural hallmarks of Baroque music. In addition, the ensemble Brecon Baroque perform with only one player per part, precisely as Bach was accustomed to doing himself.

33 Ludwig van Beethoven: *Symphony No. 5*

Orchestre Révolutionnaire et Romantique conducted by John Eliot Gardiner

Soli Deo Gloria SDG 717

With Beethoven's Symphony No. 7

If you had to pick one musical phrase in the whole of classical music known by more people than any other, it would surely be the opening two bars of

Beethoven's *Symphony No. 5*. Work on this symphony began in the early 1800s, shortly after the premiere of the mighty *'Eroica'* – a symphony similarly imbued with thrilling melodic lines from start to finish. As has been said above, there are many excellent boxed sets of the Beethoven symphonies, and if you invest in a decent one you almost certainly won't be disappointed with the interpretation of *No. 5*. But if you want a stand-alone recording of it, this is without doubt the one to get. Recorded live in concert in Carnegie Hall in 2011, it's a visceral, seat-of-your-pants performance, in which you'll hear Beethoven's music like you've never heard it before.

34 Pyotr Ilyich Tchaikovsky: *1812 Overture*
Minneapolis Symphony Orchestra conducted by Antal Doráti
Naxos 980166
With Tchaikovsky's Capriccio italien

Sadly, Tchaikovsky himself came to loathe his *1812 Overture*. It was written not through love but to fulfil a commission, and this occurred during a period of intense personal turmoil, shortly after the composer had fled to the Russian countryside to find solace following the break-up of his marriage. Given the heartache in Tchaikovsky's life at the time, it's saddening to think that he never realised how his *1812 Overture* would go on to become one of the most popular pieces of classical music. This recording dates from 1954 and features the remarkable sound of a French canon, dating from 1775 and loaned from the American military, alongside the seventy-four-bell Laura Spelman Rockefeller Memorial Carillon from Riverside Church. A simply incredible listen.

35 Nikolai Rimsky-Korsakov: *Scheherazade*

Sergei Levitin (violin). Kirov Orchestra
conducted by Valery Gergiev
Philips 470 8402
With works by Balakirev and Borodin

Nikolai Rimsky-Korsakov was an officer in the Russian navy, and one of the places he was stationed during his time at sea was, of all places, Gravesend in Kent – but that's a story for another time. He composed his epic, sea-inspired orchestral work *Scheherazade* in 1888. In this version from the Kirov Orchestra, these Russian performers play the music of their countrymen in an incisive and captivating way. Another Russian, Valery Gergiev, is on the podium; the recording was released in 2002 and it remains the most compelling and exciting rendition of this musical story of *The Arabian Nights*.

36 Sergei Rachmaninov: *Piano Concerto No. 3*

Martha Argerich (piano). Berlin Radio Symphony Orchestra conducted by Riccardo Chailly
Philips 464 7322
With Rachmaninov's Suite No. 2 for two pianos

Rachmaninov's very large hands certainly came in useful when performing this, the most technically challenging of all the composer's four piano concertos. The soloist whom Rachmaninov intended to premiere the piece was his friend Josef Hofmann; curiously, though, Hofmann never actually performed it, apparently declaring that the work was not right for him. Someone it definitely *is* right for, though, is Martha Argerich. She races through the fast passages at lightning speed, without ever missing even the smallest of details. The orchestra, meanwhile, is also on terrific form: a lesser ensemble would struggle to keep up, but the Berlin Radio Symphony Orchestra is more than up to the task.

37 Ludwig van Beethoven: *Piano Sonata No. 14 ('Moonlight')*

Steven Osborne (piano)
Hyperion CDA 67662
With three other piano sonatas by Beethoven

Despite its nickname, in Beethoven's mind this was never the *'Moonlight' Sonata*. But when the German critic Ludwig Rellstab described the sonata's famous opening movement as being akin to moonlight flickering across Lake Lucerne, he created a description that would go on to outlive the composer. Here, it's played with tenderness and deep insight by the Scottish pianist Steven Osborne. As Andrew Clements wrote in the *Guardian* when this album was released, Osborne 'does have that very special ability to make music that you thought you knew inside out seem fresh and totally alive'. That he manages to do this with one of the most famous beginnings in all classical music deserves very high praise.

38 Pyotr Ilyich Tchaikovsky:
Piano Concerto No. 1
Simon Trpčeski (piano). Royal Liverpool Philharmonic Orchestra conducted by Vasily Petrenko
Onyx 4135
With Tchaikovsky's Piano Concerto No. 2

The thunderously triumphant opening chords of this mighty concerto are instantly recognisable to most fans of classical music. At the time of composition, though, they were by no means universally loved. When Tchaikovsky played them to the pianist Nicolai Rubinstein, Rubinstein declared it to be 'bad, trivial and vulgar'. Thankfully, in the hands of the Macedonian pianist Simon Trpčeski, Rubinstein is most certainly proved wrong. This is an electrifying performance; what's more, the conductor Vasily Petrenko has a special affinity with the music of his fellow Russian, Tchaikovsky, and he brings this to the fore here with the exceptionally good Royal Liverpool Philharmonic Orchestra.

39 Ludwig van Beethoven: *Violin Concerto*
Isabelle Faust (violin). Orchestra Mozart conducted by Claudio Abbado
Harmonia Mundi HMC 902105
With Berg's Violin Concerto

When it was released in 2012, this outstanding recording of the Beethoven *Violin Concerto* received five-star reviews the world over. It was also to be one of the last recordings from the late, great conductor Claudio Abbado, who passed away at the beginning of 2014. There's a wonderful lightness of touch to Isabelle Faust's playing; in the bright, bouncy finale, in particular, it genuinely sounds as if she's having an awful lot of fun. There's also an immense depth of feeling to her playing: rich, sonorous phrases, great interplay between violin and orchestra and, overall, a mighty performance of an equally mighty work.

40 Dmitri Shostakovich: *Piano Concerto No. 2*
Dmitri Shostakovich Junior (piano). I Musici de
Montreal conducted by Maxim Shostakovich
Chandos CHAN 10565
With Shostakovich's Symphony for Strings

For the majority of his composing career,
Shostakovich wrote his music in the shadow of the
oppressive Communist regime of his day. Many of
the Russian composer's works are angst-ridden and
defiant in tone; however, his *Piano Concerto No. 2*
is a gloriously free, wistful creation – particularly in
the famous second movement, which guarantees the
work's enduring popularity. The piece was written as
a birthday present for Shostakovich's nineteen-year-
old son Maxim, himself an accomplished pianist,
and here it's *his* son, Dmitri Shostakovich Junior, at
the piano, with Maxim conducting. They're keeping
it in the family, and the result is very special indeed.

41 Tomaso Albinoni: *Adagio*
I Solisti Veneti conducted by Claudio Scimone
Erato 2292 455572
A selection of works by Albinoni and Giazotto

As you may already know, the piece we call
'Albinoni's *Adagio*' wasn't really written by the Italian
Baroque composer. Instead, it's based on a fragment
of Albinoni's music, which the Italian academic

Remo Giazzoto developed into a full work in the mid-twentieth century. At least, that's what Giazzoto originally claimed; later on in life, he changed the story, insisting that he'd written the whole thing from start to finish, without any help from his fellow Italian. However it came to be composed, this version from I Solisti Veneti under Claudio Scimone is a delight to listen to. Sonorous string sounds, and a real beauty to the playing.

42 Gabriel Fauré: *Cantique de Jean Racine*
James Vivian (organ). Choir of King's College, Cambridge, conducted by Stephen Cleobury
Decca 460 0212
A selection of choral and organ music from Allegri to Tavener (see also No. 57 below)

Gabriel Fauré was a precociously brilliant composer. By his late teens, he had already developed his own unique and utterly assured musical voice. Nowhere is this better demonstrated than in his *Cantique de Jean Racine*. Composed in 1865, when Fauré was just twenty, it's very much a precursor to his *Requiem*, with similarly intense choral writing layered on top of sparse organ accompaniment. As is so often the case with choral repertoire, we're given a first-class rendition from the Choir of King's College, Cambridge, directed by Stephen Cleobury.

Pure yet passionate singing, from a choir that can genuinely claim to be one of the finest in the world when it comes to music like this.

43 Pyotr Ilyich Tchaikovsky: *Symphony No. 6* (*'Pathétique'*)

London Philharmonic Orchestra conducted by Vladimir Jurowski

LPO 0039

With Tchaikovsky's Symphony No. 1

Was it due to cholera-infested water? Could it have been suicide? Or was it, quite simply, the result of a broken heart? All sorts of theories, both credible and anything but, have been espoused when it comes to the reason for Tchaikovsky's death in November 1893. The premiere of his *Symphony No. 6* took place just over a week before the composer's death. Of all Tchaikovsky's works, this is arguably the one that spans the extremes of the emotional spectrum to the greatest extent. In this recording, captured live in concert, the London Philharmonic Orchestra movingly conveys these extremes: electrifying moments from the brass, powerful romantic playing from the strings and an absolute commitment to the score from maestro Vladimir Jurowski all combine to make this an unforgettable performance.

44 Bedřich Smetana: *Má vlast*

Prague Philharmonia conducted by Jakub Hrůša
Supraphon SU 40322

The genre of the symphonic poem was established by the Hungarian composer Franz Liszt: a descriptive, single-movement orchestral piece, telling a story, painting a musical picture, or conveying a certain landscape. And, while Liszt was a master of the form, it was Smetana who undoubtedly composed some of the finest symphonic poems with his set entitled *Má vlast*. Given that the most famous section of the work, 'Vltava', is about the river running through Prague, it seems apt to choose this excellent recording from the Prague Philharmonia, recorded at the city's Spring Festival in 2011. It's a crystal-clear, lucid interpretation of this orchestral masterpiece.

45 Dmitri Shostakovich: 'Romance' from *The Gadfly*

Chloë Hanslip (violin). London Symphony Orchestra conducted by Paul Mann
Warner 8573 886552
A selection of short works for violin and orchestra

Although remembered principally for his large-scale orchestral works and concertos, Dmitri Shostakovich's output for the big screen was also prolific. He was, in essence, the Russian John Williams of his day: between 1929 and 1970, Shostakovich wrote more than thirty movie soundtracks. But it's his score for the 1955 film *The Gadfly* – in particular, the six-minute 'Romance' – that remains the big hit in this century. Unashamedly inspired by Massenet's soulful 'Méditation' from his opera *Thaïs*, it's an elegant melody that leans and yearns with grace and poise. The young British violinist Chloë Hanslip performs with a really innocent and beautiful tone, sympathetically accompanied by the London Symphony Orchestra.

46 George Gershwin: *Rhapsody in Blue*
André Previn (piano). London
Symphony Orchestra
Warner Classics 566 8912
With Gershwin's Concerto in F and An American in Paris

George Gershwin famously composed *Rhapsody in Blue* – or, at least, began forming ideas for the piece – while travelling on a train to Boston. To quote the composer, 'I heard it as a sort of musical kaleidoscope of America ... By the time I reached Boston I had a definite plot of the piece.' The chosen recording of the work comes from a

German-American pianist, collaborating with an English orchestra – and it's a joy from start to finish. Playful, confident and incredibly tight, this is a very assured take on Gershwin's most famous piece of music, with André Previn directing from the keyboard. What's more, if you buy the full album, you'll also get outstanding performances of Gershwin's only piano concerto and his orchestral work *An American in Paris*.

47 Sergey Prokofiev: *Romeo and Juliet*
London Symphony Orchestra conducted by
Valery Gergiev
LSO Live LSO 0682
2-CD set

The Russian conductor Valery Gergiev is one of the finest ever interpreters of the music of his fellow Russian, Sergey Prokofiev. Gergiev's concert cycle of the composer's complete symphonies with the LSO in 2004 was met with widespread acclaim, and some of his best recordings are of Prokofiev's music. This is most definitely one such example. From the opening notes of the 'Introduction', to the playfulness of *'Juliet as a Young Girl'* and the thundering opening chords of *'The Montagues and Capulets'*, the LSO is on sparkling form here. Particular praise should be given to the woodwind players, whose precision and ensemble throughout make this recording stand out all the more.

48 Giuseppe Verdi: *Nabucco*

Various soloists. Ambrosian Opera Chorus and Philharmonia Orchestra conducted by Riccardo Muti
Warner Classics 456 4472
2-CD set

Astonishing as it may be to comprehend today, when Verdi composed his opera *Nabucco* he was contemplating turning his back on the world of writing music for good. His previous opera, *Un giorno di regno*, had been panned by the critics, and he'd suffered the personal turmoil of the deaths of his wife and two children. Thankfully, he followed his agent's advice to take on a new libretto and set it to music – and the result was a roaring success. Another Italian, Riccardo Muti, here conducts the complete opera, in a performance that shimmers with passion and soul. Alternatively, if you'd like to hear it sung in English, check out David Parry's recording with the Orchestra of Opera North – part of the Chandos label's *Opera in English* series.

49 Frédéric Chopin: *Piano Concerto No. 1*

Janina Fialkowska (piano). Vancouver Symphony
Orchestra conducted by Bramwell Tovey
ATMA ACD 22643
With Chopin's Piano Concerto No. 2 (see also No. 64 below)

As you listen to this deeply expansive and expressive work, it has the mark of a composer who has
reached full emotional and musical maturity, so it's
quite something to note that Chopin wrote it while
in his late teens. In her acclaimed performance with
the Vancouver Symphony Orchestra, the Canadian
pianist Janina Fialkowska is absolutely at one with
this beautiful concerto, teasing out every ounce of
melody and romance from the score. It's also a particularly moving recording because Fialkowska had
been diagnosed with cancer of the upper arm in
2002. Operations and convalescence followed – and
this 2010 recording provided very poignant proof of
her recovery.

50 Johann Sebastian Bach: Toccata and Fugue in D minor

Simon Preston (organ)
Deutsche Grammophon E427 6682
A selection of Bach's organ music

The organist Simon Preston has had an illustrious
career, including stints at the keyboards and pedals

of Westminster Abbey and Christ Church, Oxford. His 1989 recording of some of J. S. Bach's most popular organ music, on the prestigious Deutsche Grammophon label, is still yet to be bettered – and this work, which opens the album, is the most famous of all. The *Toccata and Fugue in D minor* is a mighty piece of music, and requires something of a physical workout from the performer. As we hear on this brilliant recording, Simon Preston is more than up to the challenge.

51 Wolfgang Amadeus Mozart: *The Marriage of Figaro*

Various soloists. Choir and Orchestra of the German Opera, Berlin, conducted by Karl Böhm
Deutsche Grammophon 429 8692
3-CD set

Mozart wrote forty-one symphonies and twenty-seven piano concertos. And yet the work that said everything to him, the genre of music he truly thought to be the currency of a composer, was the opera. Mozart would have just hit thirty and had been enjoying one of his most successful periods when *The Marriage of Figaro* received its premiere. The Austrian conductor Karl Böhm, meanwhile, was well into his seventies when he led this masterful studio recording of Mozart's opera, in 1967. The performance may be nearly fifty years old now, but it's still as sparkling as ever – both in terms of the soloists' singing and the fine orchestral and choral accompaniment.

52 Carl Orff: *Carmina Burana*

Sheila Armstrong (soprano), Gerald English (tenor), Thomas Allen (baritone). St Clement Danes Grammar School Boys' Choir, London Symphony Orchestra Chorus and London Symphony Orchestra conducted by André Previn
Warner Classics 678 7042

It might be the most famous moment by far, but at less than three minutes' duration, '*O Fortuna*' is only one very small part of this mammoth, secular cantata. Composed in the 1930s and inspired by a set of medieval poems, *Carmina Burana* was first performed in Frankfurt in June 1937, to great acclaim. This recording deserves similarly high praise: Previn and his very large stage of musicians provide a compelling and jaw-dropping account of this huge work: listen out for how great the brass of the LSO sounds, in particular. If you know and love the opening of *Carmina Burana*, prepare to fall in love with the whole piece.

53 George Frideric Handel: *Solomon*
Various soloists. Gabrieli Consort and Players
conducted by Paul McCreesh
Deutsche Grammophon Archiv 459 6882
3-CD set

The regular inclusion of Handel's oratorio *Solomon* in the Classic FM Hall of Fame is due in large part to one section: *'The Arrival of the Queen of Sheba'*, a three-minute lesson in how to compose a great Baroque tune. But the entire oratorio is definitely worth exploring – and there can be no better way to do that than with this excellent release from the expert Handelian Paul McCreesh. His star line-up of soloists includes the counter-tenor Andreas Scholl and the soprano Susan Gritton, and their performances, coupled with the zesty playing of the Gabrieli Consort and Players, make for a vivid and arresting interpretation of this fine oratorio.

54 Edvard Grieg: *Peer Gynt Suites*
Estonian National Symphony Orchestra
conducted by Paavo Järvi
Erato Classics 545 7222

Grieg's *Peer Gynt* came about after the composer was commissioned by the playwright Henrik Ibsen to set to music his quintessentially Scandinavian play of the same name. Grieg responded by creating a collection of tableaux, some of which were later formed into two separate suites. He didn't have much faith in them, feeling under pressure from Ibsen to come up with the melodies as quickly as possible, but they were received with huge enthusiasm by the Norwegian audiences of his day. Given that the two suites are Grieg's own distillation of the best moments, it's not surprising that they quickly became more popular than the complete score. Here, the Estonian National Symphony Orchestra offers an excellent account of both suites, under the watchful eye of Paavo Järvi.

55 Giuseppe Verdi: *Requiem*

Anja Harteros (soprano), Sonia Ganassi
(mezzo-soprano), Rolando Villazon (tenor),
René Pape (bass). Orchestra and Chorus of
the National Academy of St Cecilia conducted
by Antonio Pappano
Warner Classics 698 9362
2-CD set

At the release of this recording in 2009, the great conductor Antonio Pappano commented: 'I love doing this piece here in Rome with an Italian chorus and an Italian orchestra, and they have an innate sense of what this music is about, how to bring it to life. They really know what the words mean. They have lived what it is like to be religious or spiritual in Italy.' Listen to this incredibly good recording, and you'll get a sense of just what Pappano means. The fiery 'Dies Irae' is simply thrilling, the soloists are at the top of their game, and the chorus is on genuinely stunning form. This is a Verdi *Requiem* to treasure, and to return to again and again.

56 Johann Sebastian Bach: *Brandenburg Concertos*
European Brandenburg Ensemble
conducted by Trevor Pinnock
Avie AV 2119
2-CD *set*

In 2008, the celebrated British conductor Trevor Pinnock handpicked a select group of musicians from across Europe, all of whom were known for their expertise in performing music from the Baroque period. He named this new group the European Brandenburg Ensemble, and set about recording Bach's six *Brandenburg Concertos* with them. The result is jam-packed with infectious musicality, first-rate playing and an almost relent-less exuberance. Pinnock had already recorded these concertos a quarter of a century earlier, and here he returns to them with added insight, creating a fantastic collection of one of Bach's finest works.

57 Charles-Marie Widor: 'Toccata' from Organ Symphony No. 5
Stephen Cleobury (organ)
Decca 460 0212
A selection of choral and organ music from Allegri to Tavener (see also No. 42 above)

The French composer Charles-Marie Widor wrote a total of ten organ symphonies – but sadly, it is only the 'Toccata' from *No. 5* that retains any kind of popular appeal today. It's quite some popular appeal, though, being one of the most regularly requested wedding-day pieces in the world, with many a bride and groom having left the church to the sound of 'the Widor', as it is often called. Widor himself was a master of the instrument (he succeeded his fellow French composer César Franck as Professor of Organ at the Paris Conservatoire), as is the organist and choral music expert Stephen Cleobury. His version of the 'Toccata' is crisp, clear and immensely rewarding – whether or not you happen to be walking down the aisle any time soon.

58 Pyotr Ilyich Tchaikovsky: *Swan Lake*
Orchestra of the Mariinsky Theatre conducted
by Valery Gergiev
Decca 475 7669
2-CD set

Tchaikovsky evidently enjoyed composing the music
for *Swan Lake*, writing far more material than would
ever be required. Indeed, the version most com-
monly encountered today is, in fact, an edited one,
created after the composer's death and consider-
ably shorter than the original, full-length work. It's
now the world's most frequently performed ballet;
and it's not surprising that the chosen recording
is an all-Russian one, from the Orchestra of the
Mariinsky Theatre and the star conductor Valery
Gergiev. There's so much to enjoy here, from the
graceful *Waltz* in Act 1 to the playful *'Dance of the
Cygnets'*. Highly recommended.

59 George Frideric Handel: *Zadok the Priest*
The Sixteen and The Sixteen Orchestra
conducted by Harry Christophers
Coro COR 16066
*With other Coronation music by Handel and extracts
from Messiah*

We're very proud to be able to call The Sixteen 'The
Voices of Classic FM'. For over a decade now, we've

worked with this world-class ensemble to bring choral music to the widest possible audience across the UK, and it's therefore great to be able to shine the spotlight on this, one of their finest recordings. The singing in *Zadok the Priest* is exemplary; the added bonus of this recording is that on the full album, you'll also find outstanding versions of Handel's other Coronation Anthems. The Sixteen are always on particularly strong form when performing music of the Renaissance and Baroque periods – and this recording is certainly no exception.

60 Richard Strauss: *Four Last Songs*

Nina Stemme (soprano). Orchestra of the Royal Opera House, Covent Garden, conducted by Antonio Pappano
Warner Classics 3787972
With arias from Capriccio and Salome

For many people, Jessye Norman's recording of the *Four Last Songs* is *the* one to get hold of. Certainly, her rendition of the fourth song – *'At Dusk'* – is sublime. But there's a version from 2007 which, dare I say it, beats even the mighty Ms Norman's: namely, this one from the Swedish soprano Nina Stemme. It's not just her performance that's deeply moving; the orchestral playing is also radiant. Antonio Pappano made a very good point at the time of the record's release: 'I trust the warmth of Nina's voice. There are a lot of lighter voices that have recorded the piece but you have to remember that Kirsten Flagstad sang at the premiere and it's that kind of ample voice with warmth and body – Nina's voice – that I think is too rarely heard in this repertoire.'

61 Giacomo Puccini: *Madam Butterfly*

Angela Gheorghiu (soprano), Jonas Kaufmann (tenor). Orchestra and Chorus of the National Academy of St Cecilia conducted by Antonio Pappano

Warner Classics 264 18728

2-CD *set*

Hundreds of operas have tragedy at their core, but you would be hard pushed to find a more perfect example of this theme expressed in music than Puccini's masterful *Madam Butterfly*. It was a personal favourite of the composer, too: he once described it as 'the most felt and most expressive opera that I have conceived'. Angela Gheorghiu and Jonas Kaufmann are two of opera's most in-demand stars on the world stage, and they here join forces with another operatic *tour de force*, the conductor Antonio Pappano. The full recording is worth buying for Gheorghiu's performance of *'Un Bel Di'* alone: simply beautiful.

62 Felix Mendelssohn: *Hebrides Overture ('Fingal's Cave')*

Vienna Philharmonic Orchestra conducted by
Christian Thielemann
Deutsche Grammophon 474 5022
A selection of overtures by German composers

How do you conjure up the sights and sounds of Scotland in a single piece of music? That was the challenge facing Felix Mendelssohn when, in 1829, he travelled home from a memorable trip to the Scottish island of Staffa and its famous Fingal's Cave. Just hours after getting home, he had written the first few bars, and this part of the UK clearly had a significant effect on the young composer. On this recording from the Vienna Phil, the woodwind section is on particularly fine form, evocatively conveying the weather on Staffa, while the shimmering strings also play a large part in making this a captivating performance.

63 Wolfgang Amadeus Mozart: *The Magic Flute*

Barbara Hendricks (soprano), June Anderson (soprano),
Thomas Allen (baritone), Robert Lloyd (bass),
Alistair Miles (bass). Scottish Chamber Orchestra
and Chorus conducted by Charles Mackerras
Telarc 89408 03022
2-CD set

Often referred to by many as Mozart's only

pantomime, *The Magic Flute* is a riot of life, lust and ludicrous plot. This particular recording, which dates from 1992, features the much missed conductor Charles Mackerras at the helm of an impressive cast, who collectively manage to capture Mozart's heady mix of farce, high drama and magic. The Scottish Chamber Orchestra – an ensemble with whom Mackerras made so many fine recordings – is on very bright form here, drawing us in at the opening 'Overture' and remaining alert and responsive throughout. And the singing from both chorus and soloists is first rate.

64 Frédéric Chopin: *Piano Concerto No. 2*
    Janina Fialkowska (piano).
    Vancouver Symphony Orchestra
    conducted by Bramwell Tovey
    ATMA ACD 22643
    With Chopin's Piano Concerto No. 1 (see also
    No. 49 above)

This recording has already been mentioned, in the context of Chopin's *Piano Concerto No. 1* (which he actually composed *after* his *Piano Concerto No. 2* – but that's a story for another day). I make no apology for including it again here, for, once again, this is playing of immense beauty and tenderness.

The concerto is an astonishing work for a composer so young (bear in mind: Chopin was barely out of his teens when he wrote it) and Janina Fialkowska manages to convey some of that innocence in her playing, while also bringing to bear her mature, thoughtful interpretation of the piece. Once again, the orchestra is on top form, too.

65 Franz Schubert: *Piano Quintet ('Trout')*
   Clifford Curzon (piano). Amadeus Quartet
   BBC Legends 40092
   With Brahms' F minor Piano Quintet

The English pianist Clifford Curzon was one of the finest pianists of his generation. He died over thirty years ago now – so, in comparison to many other recordings in this book, any recommendations featuring him are relatively old. But this one is an absolute gem, which has arguably yet to be bettered. Curzon's playing is fizzing with energy, wit and grace, and there's wonderful interplay between him and the members of the Amadeus Quartet. Chamber music was essentially conceived as being 'music with friends', and there's no better example of that than this recording.

66 Claude Debussy: *Suite bergamasque*

Pascal Rogé (piano)

Onyx 4018

*The second disc in a series of Debussy's
complete piano music, with Children's Corner
and Estampes*

There are many fine recordings of Debussy's *Suite bergamasque*, from which the famous 'Clair de Lune' is taken, and a great deal of these are by French pianists. Jean-Efflam Bavouzet's account is well worth discovering, as is Jean-Yves Thibaudet's – but the one that trumps them all is arguably this recording from Pascal Rogé. He really understands Debussy's music: it's dreamy without being dense, and there's a beautiful flow in his phrasing. The sound quality here is excellent, too. When Debussy wrote the *Suite bergamasque*, he was going through a tough time, struggling to make ends meet as a composer. Today, it's one of his most enduring works – and you won't find a better interpretation of it than this one.

67 Wolfgang Amadeus Mozart: *Flute and Harp Concerto*

Emmanuel Pahud (flute), Marie-Pierre Langlamet (harp). Berlin Philharmonic Orchestra conducted by Claudio Abbado

Warner Classics 085 1952

With Mozart's Flute Concerto No. 1 and Clarinet Concerto

There is a wonderful scene – one of many – in the 1984 film *Amadeus*, in which the jealous Salieri sees the score of Mozart's *Flute and Harp Concerto* and is simply bowled over, incredulous at how divine the melody and orchestration are. And he's right. The central slow movement must surely be one of the most glorious melodies not just in Mozart's output but, possibly, in all music. And in this account featuring Emmanuel Pahud and Marie-Pierre Langlamet, it simply radiates warmth. There's a genuine dialogue between the soloists, which, when combined with very sympathetic accompaniment from the Berlin Philharmonic Orchestra, creates a beautiful version of an equally beautiful work.

68 Giacomo Puccini: *La bohème*

Anna Netrebko (soprano), Rolando Villazon
(tenor), Boaz Daniel (baritone). Children's Choir
of the Gartnerplatz State Theatre and Bavarian
Radio Symphony Orchestra conducted by
Bertrand de Billy
Deutsche Grammophon 477 6600
2-CD set

Studio recordings of operas are often glorious –
indeed, some have already been highly praised in
these pages – but there's something very special
about listening to a performance that was recorded
live in front of an audience. This version of Puccini's
La bohème, recorded in Munich in April 2007, features the dream partnership of Anna Netrebko and
Rolando Villazon. Some would argue that, eight
years on, Villazon is no longer at the top of his
game but here his talents are unmistakable. The
role of Rodolfo sounds as if it was written for him,
and Anna Netrebko's Mimi is vulnerable yet wholly
assured. Add to that a first-class orchestra, and you
have a recording that's unmissable.

69 Jean Sibelius: *Symphony No. 5*

City of Birmingham Symphony Orchestra
conducted by Simon Rattle
Warner Classics 503 43282
With Nielsen's Symphony No. 4

Sibelius premiered his Fifth Symphony on
8 December 1915 – his fiftieth birthday, as it hap-
pens. Along with the Second Symphony, *Finlandia*
and the *Karelia Suite*, it sits as one of the composer's
finest and most loved orchestral works, and in the
hands of Simon Rattle and the CBSO, this symphony is simply electrifying. As well as purchasing
the symphony on one, stand-alone album, it's also
available as part of a complete set – all featuring
the same performers, and also including a brilliant
performance of the composer's *Violin Concerto* with
Nigel Kennedy as soloist. Either way, you won't be
disappointed; this is fabulous music-making.

70 Jules Massenet: 'Méditation' from *Thaïs*

Maxim Vengerov (violin). Virtuosi directed by
Vag Papian
Warner Classics CDC 557 1642
A selection of violin favourites

Even among a group of classical music experts,
you'd be hard pushed to find anyone who could
instantly tell you the plot of French composer

Jules Massenet's relatively unknown opera *Thaïs*. Instead, the work's popularity, longevity and wide appeal are down not to anything particularly operatic, but to a six-minute instrumental section that is heard during a scene change. In that sense, the beautiful 'Méditation' for solo violin and orchestra is officially an intermezzo in opera-speak. Far from being filler music, it's a captivating, pure performance piece in its own right. And that's exactly what we get here, from the gloriously pure-toned Maxim Vengerov and the ensemble Virtuosi.

71 Wolfgang Amadeus Mozart: *Ave, verum Corpus*
The Sixteen and Academy of St Martin in the Fields conducted by Harry Christophers
Coro COR 16057
With Fauré's Requiem and Mozart's Vespers (K339)

Just forty-six bars containing around three minutes of music. And yet they are capable of leaving the listener just as moved as might an entire five-day-long cycle of Wagner's *The Ring*. And certainly less tired. *Ave, verum Corpus* is another work that Mozart composed in the final year of his life; it was written for a small-town choir, which perhaps explains its relative yet magical simplicity. Once again, The Voices of Classic FM, The Sixteen, provide the chosen recording; their crystal-clear diction, united approach and heavenly singing combine to create a recording of which Mozart himself would have surely approved.

72 Wolfgang Amadeus Mozart: *Solemn Vespers*
**Various soloists. Winchester Cathedral Choir
and Academy of Ancient Music conducted by
Christopher Hogwood**
Warner Classics 2564 6011912
With other sacred music by Mozart

These *Vespers* are one of a pair. They come alongside the *Solemn Vespers for Sunday*, and the reason for this first set's popularity rests on one five-minute section: the beautiful 'Laudate Dominum'. On this excellent recording, it's sung by the peerless Emma Kirkby – often praised for her interpretations of Baroque music, but equally fine when tackling the music of Mozart. There's great purity from the Winchester Cathedral Choir, too – and they're an apt ensemble to include, given that this piece offers one of the best examples of Mozart's religious music. Christopher Hogwood, meanwhile, faithfully interprets the composer's score, bringing finesse and clarity with the excellent Academy of Ancient Music.

73 Ludwig van Beethoven:

Symphony No. 3 ('Eroica')

Anima Eterna conducted by Jos van Immerseel

Zig Zag ZZT 804026

With Beethoven's overtures Coriolan and Egmont,
and The Ruins of Athens, the second of a 6-CD set of
Beethoven's complete symphonies and overtures

First of all, a disclaimer: not everyone will love this recording. Is it indisputably the finest recording of Beethoven's *'Eroica'*, ever? No. But will it make you listen to this groundbreaking symphony in a fresh, exciting way? Absolutely. After picking so many recordings by well-known symphony orchestras, now it seems right to choose something a little different that will help you hear Beethoven differently. The *'Eroica'* ushered in the start of the Romantic period – and here, the symphony is performed on period instruments. In other words, instruments that were used in the composer's own lifetime. To quote the conductor Jos van Immerseel, 'We know that Beethoven asked musicians very precise questions about the technical capabilities of their instruments. So he knew exactly what he was doing when he pushed an instrument to the very limit of its possibilities … That's why it's so important to perform the music on period instruments.' You be the judge, as you listen to this vivid, raw and very impressive recording.

74 Wolfgang Amadeus Mozart:
Eine kleine Nachtmusik
Chamber Players of Canada
ATMA ACD 22532
With Mozart's Piano Concertos Nos 13 and 14, and Variations on 'Ah vous dirai-je, maman'

Despite possessing a brain that could remember music with 100 per cent precision, Mozart kept a detailed log of everything he'd written, just in case. The title 'Eine kleine Nacht musik' is what he jotted down next to the entry for this particular serenade, written for a string quartet with an added double-bass. This recording showcases the talents of the Ottawa-based Chamber Players of Canada. Released in 2013, it's a pared-back recording (many of the versions of this work are played by a larger ensemble, even though that's not what Mozart asked for). What's more, the album features a couple of arrangements of two early Mozart piano concertos – Nos 13 and 14 with soloist Janina Fialkowska (see entries 49 and 64) – which provide a welcome opportunity to discover some of the composer's lesser-known music.

75 Pyotr Ilyich Tchaikovsky: *Symphony No. 5*
Bavarian Radio Symphony Orchestra
conducted by Mariss Jansons
BR Klassik 900105
With Tchaikovsky's Francesca da Rimini

When Tchaikovsky composed his Fifth Symphony, a decade had passed since the fairly unsuccessful premiere of his *Symphony No. 4* (admittedly punctuated by the composition of the *Manfred Symphony* in 1885) and Tchaikovsky worked painstakingly hard to ensure that his latest symphonic creation received a favourable response. Sadly, the reaction to this four-movement work was, at best, muted. But when you listen to this glistening account of it from the Bavarian Radio Symphony Orchestra under Mariss Jansons, it's very hard to fathom why. Tchaikovsky's great skill as an orchestrator is spotlighted brilliantly well here, with perky woodwind playing, luxurious strings and mightily clear moments from the brass.

76 Gustav Mahler: *Symphony No. 2*
('Resurrection')

Eteri Gvazava (soprano), Anna Larsson (contralto).
Orféon Donostiarra and the Lucerne Festival
Orchestra conducted by Claudio Abbado
Deutsche Grammophon 477 0582
2-CD set, with Debussy's La Mer

Mahler clearly fancied a challenge when composing his *Symphony No. 2* in the late 1800s. His
triumphant symphonic debut, the *'Titan'*, had
called for many more instruments than was the
norm, so for his follow-up he decided to go one
step further. The gargantuan symphony orchestra would remain, but alongside it was placed
an organ, an offstage brass ensemble, and some
church bells. And a choir. A very large choir. And,
to round things off, some soloists. Performing the
work is therefore hugely ambitious – and managing
to pull off a truly great recording is even more of
a challenge. On every front, Claudio Abbado and
his enormous ensemble of musicians succeed, in
this mighty interpretation.

77 Jean Sibelius: *Karelia Suite*

Philharmonia Orchestra conducted by
Vladimir Ashkenazy
Decca 455 4022
With Sibelius's Symphony Nos 1, 2 and 4
and Finlandia (as single disc)

This is certainly a very fine recording of one of
Sibelius's most famous works. The Philharmonia
Orchestra sounds utterly at home under the baton
of Vladimir Ashkenazy, and its ability to portray the
nationalistic fervour at the heart of the suite is commendable. But what also makes this one stand out
is that it is, quite frankly, a bargain. It's part of a
series called 'Double Decca' – which, as the name
would suggest, offers two CDs at a special price.
In this case, for little more than the cost of a coffee
(albeit a rather large coffee, and maybe a muffin
on the side) you get not just the *Karelia Suite* but
also *Finlandia* and *Symphonies Nos 1, 2* and *4*. All
expertly performed, too.

78 Johann Sebastian Bach: *St Matthew Passion*

Various soloists. Vienna Boys' Choir, Arnold
Schoenberg Choir and Concentus Musicus Vienna
conducted by Nikolaus Harnoncourt
Teldec 2564 643472
3-CD set

Bach's *St Matthew Passion* was a very ambitious
work in the composer's own day – requiring, as it
does, two separate orchestras – and it remains one
of his crowning glories. There are many fine recordings of it, principally from Baroque specialists, and
the chosen version is a very special interpretation
under the baton of the Austrian conductor Nikolaus
Harnoncourt. There's a pared-down sound to the
chorus, which has significantly fewer members than
is the case on many other versions, and every soloist demonstrates exquisite moments of colour and
beauty. There's a great acoustic, too, and Concentus
Musicus Vienna provides excellent accompaniment
throughout.

79 Aram Khachaturian: *'Adagio of Spartacus and Phrygia'* from *Spartacus*

Bournemouth Symphony Orchestra conducted by Kirill Karabits

Onyx 4063

With extracts from Khachaturian's Gayaneh

'Not a hair of a note was out of place; this was a performance by a world-class orchestra.' So said *The Times* about the Bournemouth Symphony Orchestra, in a review that was published not long after the arrival of the star Russian conductor Kirill Karabits in the seaside town. In recent years, Karabits' leadership of Classic FM's Orchestra in the South of England has been incredibly exciting, and this recording of music by Khachaturian is captivating. It contains a suite that includes the perennially popular *'Adagio of Spartacus and Phrygia'*, made famous to millions when it was used as the theme tune to the TV series *The Onedin Line* in the 1970s and '80s.

80 Maurice Ravel: *Boléro*

Boston Symphony Orchestra conducted by
Seiji Ozawa
Deutsche Grammophon 415 8452
*With Ravel's Ma Mère l'oye, Rapsodie espagnole and
other orchestral music*

Ravel's famous *Boléro* is definitely one of those
'Marmite' pieces of music: you either love it or hate
it. If you're in the latter camp, skip past this entry
to discover some more sumptuous Sibelius to add to
your collection; if, meanwhile, you're in the former,
you should definitely get hold of this fine recording from the Boston Symphony Orchestra under
Seiji Ozawa. The dynamic range in this piece – from
ultra-quiet at the start through to super-loud at the
end – is very skilfully handled here, and the tightly
knit orchestral playing ensures a wonderful unity
of sound.

81 Jean Sibelius: *Symphony No. 2*

London Symphony Orchestra conducted by
Colin Davis
LSO Live 0605
With Pohjola's Daughter

The late British conductor Colin Davis was a very
unassuming fellow. Once, after being interviewed
here at Classic FM, one of our presenters asked if

his driver was collecting him. 'My driver?' he scoffed. 'Of course not! I'm off to John Lewis to buy some wool, so I can do some knitting when I get home!' His modest, quiet manner belied a steely vision and power as a conductor, brought to the fore in this fantastic recording of Sibelius. There's an added thrill due to the fact that this is a live, in-concert performance, recorded at London's Barbican in 2006. The majestic sound world Sibelius inhabits is beautifully conveyed here; the finale, in particular, is simply spellbinding.

82 Johannes Brahms: *Violin Concerto*
Vadim Repin (violin). Leipzig Gewandhaus
Orchestra conducted by Riccardo Chailly
Deutsche Grammophon 477 7470
With Brahms' Double Concerto
for violin and cello

Brahms lived and worked under the shadow of Beethoven throughout his career – and in the case of this violin concerto, there's an obvious parallel to be made between the composers' works. Vadim Repin's recording of the Beethoven is certainly very fine – but it's with the music of Brahms that he absolutely shines. He completely understands how to contrast the raw and rugged sound of the outer movements with an Adagio of exquisite beauty, performing with an intimacy that is truly moving. With first-class accompaniment from the Leipzig Gewandhaus Orchestra, and a maestro as incisive as Riccardo Chailly, this is a recording to treasure.

83 Jean Sibelius: *Violin Concerto*

Pinchas Zukerman (violin). London Philharmonic Orchestra conducted by Daniel Barenboim
Deutsche Grammophon 479 3772
With Brahms' Violin Concerto

Today, we know Sibelius as a composer – but at the start of his career, he was very much a violinist, first and foremost. So it's no surprise that his *Violin Concerto* is expertly composed for the instrument. Pretty much all of the world's finest violinists have this one in their repertoire. Although, given how muscular the piece is, it's often not one that soloists tackle first off. This particular recording was made in the 1970s, when both Pinchas Zukerman and Daniel Barenboim were considered as being among the most exciting young musicians on the planet. Their youthful vitality, combined with a tremendous energy, makes this a very special recording.

84 Pyotr Ilyich Tchaikovsky: *Violin Concerto*
Anne-Sophie Mutter (violin). Vienna Philharmonic
Orchestra conducted by André Previn
Deutsche Grammophon 474 8742
With Korngold's Violin Concerto

Along with the violin concertos of Bruch and
Mendelssohn, this warhorse by Tchaikovsky is one
of the most important works for the instrument in
the history of Romantic music. This album, released
in 2004, contains Mutter's second recording of the
work. It was made with her then husband, André
Previn, and it contains ample proof that both soloist and conductor totally understand the concerto's
full-blooded romance. Tchaikovsky was apparently
going to dedicate the piece to one of his pupils, the
violinist Joseph Kotek, but, only too aware of the
rumours surrounding Kotek's sexuality, he ultimately
chose not to. As he confided to his publisher, this
was 'in order to avoid gossip of various kinds'.

85 Johann Strauss II: *By the Beautiful Blue Danube*
Berlin Philharmonic Orchestra conducted by
Herbert von Karajan
Deutsche Grammophon 477 7341
2-CD set of Karajan's career highlights

Many people would think it rather odd that the
chosen recording of this piece isn't one that features

the Vienna Philharmonic Orchestra. After all, *By the Beautiful Blue Danube* is synonymous with the famous New Year's Day Concert in Vienna, the live recording of which is released each year. Certainly, there are countless fine performances of the piece recorded on that annual occasion – but the version chosen above is worth getting hold of largely because it showcases the most recorded conductor in the history of classical music: Herbert von Karajan. Released to coincide with the centenary of his birth, this album contains many of the conductor's most popular recordings, including a lilting, lyrical version of this ever-popular waltz.

86 Giuseppe Verdi: *La traviata*

Maria Callas (soprano), Francesco Albanese (tenor), Ugo Savarese (baritone). RAI Chorus and Orchestra of Turin conducted by Gabriele Santini
Warner Classics 2564 634085
2-CD set

Maria Callas was arguably the greatest soprano of the twentieth century, and this performance of *La traviata* was her only studio recording of Verdi's most famous opera. It was made in 1953, and in the autumn of 2014 Warner Classics released this remastered version, which cannot be recommended highly enough. The original recording was made when Callas was at the height of her fame (between 1951 and 1958, she performed the role of Violetta more than sixty times) and, over well over half a century later, she has yet to be bettered. The orchestral playing, and the performances from the other soloists, are commendable, too – but this recording is well worth buying for Callas alone.

87 Jay Ungar: *The Ashokan Farewell*
John Perkins (violin). Band of
Her Majesty's Royal Marines
Classic FM CFMCD 4

When we began playing *The Ashokan Farewell* on Classic FM during the early years of the twenty-first century, it was very quickly clear that we had a hit on our hands. Our switchboard lit up every time we gave it a spin – and today, it's a firm fixture in the Classic FM Hall of Fame. Unlike with many of the pieces in this book, picking out the best recording of *The Ashokan Farewell* is a very simple affair. The reason? Quite simply, it's the one that introduced the work to us in the first place. Major John Perkins leads the Band of Her Majesty's Royal Marines from the violin in this beguiling and beautiful melody.

88 Johann Sebastian Bach: *Mass in B minor*

Various soloists. Collegium Vocale Orchestra
and Collegium Vocale of Gent conducted by
Philippe Herreweghe
PHI LPH012
2-CD set

There are several reasons why many Bach lovers
regard the *Mass in B minor* as the pinnacle of his
work. Size, for one, singles it out, even when com-
pared with his previous titans, the *St John Passion*
and *St Matthew Passion*. Composed during 1748
and 1749, it came at the end of Bach's life (he
died in July 1750) and it's a deeply moving piece
of music. The Baroque music specialist Philippe
Herreweghe has so far made three separate recordings of the *Mass in B minor*, and this one is far
and away the best. The soloists blend perfectly, the
interpretation is ever faithful to the score, and the
beauty of Bach's music is wonderfully conveyed.

89 Pyotr Ilyich Tchaikovsky: *The Nutcracker*

Kirov Orchestra conducted by Valery Gergiev
Philips 462 1142

Audiences in St Petersburg were promised 'a fairy-
tale ballet' in the winter of 1892 when, all around the
city, posters began to appear advertising the much

anticipated new project from Tchaikovsky. He had been commissioned to set to music a popular family story called *The Nutcracker and the Mouse-King*, a festive favourite that begins on Christmas Eve in the house of two young children, Clara and Fritz. There's a wonderfully vivid, pictorial quality to Tchaikovsky's music and here the recording from the Kirov Orchestra under Valery Gergiev embodies exactly those qualities, too. These Russian players clearly know their countryman's music incredibly well; it's a delight to listen to.

90 Modest Mussorgsky: *Pictures at an Exhibition*

Steven Osborne (piano)
Hyperion CDA 67896
With Prokofiev's Sarcasms and Visions fugitives

Ravel orchestration:
Oslo Philharmonic Orchestra conducted by
Mariss Jansons
Warner Classics 350 8242
With Mussorgsky's Night on the Bare Mountain

Modest Mussorgsky was good friends with a painter called Vladimir Hartmann. Tragically, Hartmann died at the peak of his career, aged just thirty-nine, and the loss of not just a close friend but an artistic inspiration had a deep effect on the composer. By way of a tribute, he decided to write a set of piano pieces, inspired by an exhibition of the artist's work that Mussorgsky had visited after his friend's death. These pieces are played with sensitivity and virtuosity by the Scottish pianist Steven Osborne, but today, Maurice Ravel's orchestrated version of *Pictures at an Exhibition* is performed more frequently than the piano version. And if it's the full orchestra you're after, you can't go wrong with the Oslo Philharmonic.

91 Edward Elgar: *The Dream of Gerontius*

Alice Coote (mezzo-soprano), Paul Groves (tenor),
Bryn Terfel (bass-baritone). Hallé Orchestra,
Hallé Choir and Hallé Youth Choir conducted by
Mark Elder
Hallé CDHLD 7520
2-CD set

Having already sung the praises of the conductor Mark Elder, who's indisputably one of the finest modern-day interpreters of the music of Elgar, it's no surprise to find him at the helm of this recording, too. *The Dream of Gerontius* is arguably the finest choral work ever to have come out of England – and this all-British recording of it is one to enjoy again and again. In May 2008, around the time that this recording was made, the *Guardian* wrote of the Hallé that 'the golden era may be happening right now'; the following year, this recording won a prestigious Classic FM Gramophone Award. Powerful singing from chorus and soloists alike, coupled with a rich, rewarding sound from the orchestra, combine to create the finest recording of *The Dream of Gerontius* in modern times.

92 Richard Wagner: *Tristan and Isolde*

Nina Stemme (soprano), Placido Domingo (tenor), Ian Bostridge (tenor). Orchestra and Chorus of the Royal Opera House, Covent Garden, conducted by Antonio Pappano

Warner Classics 58006

3-CD set

Wagner himself described this opera as a tale of 'the bliss and wretchedness of love', and one that could end only with 'one sole redemption – death'. Most famous for its Prelude, in which we find the much analysed '*Tristan* Chord' – which was to confound and fascinate critics and musicologists in equal measure – *Tristan and Isolde* is an opera on an absolutely epic scale. The great tenor Placido Domingo (now more comfortable as a baritone) recorded this in his sixties; despite his advancing years, his voice has lost none of its power. By contrast, it has a richness and a maturity that is perfectly suited to Wagner's music. Add Nina Stemme and the Orchestra of the Royal Opera House, and you have a simply superb interpretation of Wagner's most famous opera.

93 Franz Schubert: *String Quintet in C*
Mstislav Rostropovich (cello). Melos Quartet
Deutsche Grammophon 477 6357

Franz Schubert's beautiful *String Quintet in C* is a rather poignant work: the composer never truly realised how popular it would become and, within just a couple of months of its composition, he had died. Today, it is recognised as one of his most tender creations, with an Adagio of exquisite beauty – and in this recording from the great Russian cellist Mstislav Rostropovich and the Melos Quartet, Schubert's music is in perfect hands. The glorious tone from Rostropovich seems to ground the ensemble throughout; in addition to their nuanced interpretation of the most tender moments, they are also absolutely at one in the more intense outer movements of the quintet.

94 Richard Wagner: *Tannhäuser*

Various soloists. Bayreuth Festival Orchestra and
Chorus conducted by Wolfgang Sawallisch
Orfeo C888143D
3-CD set

In 1961, a brand new cast assembled to perform
Wagner's great opera *Tannhäuser* at the famous
Bayreuth Festival. Unfortunately, as is often the case
on these occasions, the opening night wasn't exactly a
resounding success – a point the critics drove home
soon after. However, this production of *Tannhäuser*
would go on to become the hottest ticket in town –
so, when a recording of the next performance was
discovered, there was much excitement. This very
recording was re-released in September 2014, featuring an all-star cast including the soloists Dietrich
Fischer-Dieskau and Victoria de los Angeles. It may
be over half a century old, but it remains a must-have
for any lover of Wagner's music.

95 Giuseppe Verdi: *Aida*

Leontyne Price (soprano), Robert Merrill
(baritone), Jon Vickers (tenor). Rome Opera
Orchestra and Chorus conducted by Georg Solti
Decca 460 7652
2-CD set

For many people, a knowledge of Verdi's *Aida* doesn't

stretch much further than the triumphant *Grand March*, which features in Act II of the opera. But it's definitely worth discovering *Aida* in its entirety – and there's no better way to do it than through this landmark studio recording dating from 1961. The fantastic Leontyne Price very much leads the way here, but her fellow soloists were also at the top of their game when this recording was made. They were all being booked to perform Verdi's music in the world's most famous opera houses, and getting them together on this one recording would have been no mean feat. Highly recommended.

96 Léo Delibes: *Lakmé*

Various soloists. Toulouse Capitole Choir and
Orchestra conducted by Michel Plasson
Warner Classics CDS 5565692
2-CD *set*

Most of us would be hard pressed to describe the characters, plot or musical development of Delibes' three-act opera *Lakmé*. Its resurgent popularity in the 1990s was down to one thing: the use of one particular section of the opera in a certain television commercial. The *Flower Duet* first appeared in a British Airways advert in 1989 and quickly became one of the most well-known pieces of classical music in Britain. On this recording, that duet is expertly sung by Natalie Dessay and Delphine Haidan – but there's so much more to discover, too. The French conductor Michel Plasson is the ideal interpreter of Delibes' sumptuous, exotic music, and he leads the Toulouse Capitole Choir and Orchestra with panache.

97 Richard Wagner: *Die Walküre*

Various soloists. Bayreuth Festival Orchestra conducted by Daniel Barenboim
Teldec 4509 911862
4-CD set

At around five hours in duration, Wagner's opera *Die Walküre* is an epic work – but, like the opera described above from Delibes, most people know of it only because of a single five-minute section. In this case, it's *The Ride of the Valkyries*, but once again, there are many reasons to dive into the entire opera, rather than only ever cherry-picking that one section. Daniel Barenboim is one of the greatest living Wagnerians – and with a cast that includes the peerless John Tomlinson as Wotan, you know you're on to an absolute winner. If you buy it, but you don't have five hours spare to listen to the whole thing, give *Wotan's Farewell* a listen. You'll be instantly hooked – guaranteed.

98 Antonín Dvořák: *Cello Concerto*

Alisa Weilerstein (cello). Czech Philharmonic
Orchestra conducted by Jiří Bělohlávek
Decca 478 5705
With short works by Dvořák for cello and piano

There are many outstanding recordings of this,
the second-most-performed cello concerto in the
world (no prizes for guessing that Elgar composed
the most popular one) – not least the legendary
performance from Mstislav Rostropovich and the
Berlin Philharmonic Orchestra under Herbert
von Karajan. But this chosen version is a compara-
tively recent one, having been released in spring
2014. It features the dazzling young American
cellist Alisa Weilerstein, who's been wowing the
critics for several years now. Her recording of the
Elgar concerto catapulted her to stardom but her
take on the Dvořák is arguably an even better interpretation of the composer's intentions.

99 Georges Bizet: *Carmen*

Various soloists. French National Orchestra and the
Chorus of Radio France conducted by Lorin Maazel
Erato 2292 452072
3-CD set

Bizet's two famous operas couldn't be more different. The first, *The Pearl Fishers*, is remembered for

containing only one real hit. *Carmen*, by contrast, is so packed full of memorable melodies that it's guaranteed an almost permanent position as the world's most popular and most frequently performed opera. From the barnstorming orchestral *Prelude* to the macho *Toreador Song*, via the sexy *Habanera* and the sultry *Seguidilla*, this is like a nineteenth-century collection of three-minute pop songs from start to finish. In this French recording of the work (albeit with an American conductor), every moment of *Carmen* is one to relish. Bizet composed mass-market music in the very best sense of that phrase – and it's music you won't hear performed better than in the hands of these performers.

100 George Frideric Handel: *Water Music Suites*
Zefiro conducted by Alfredo Bernadini
Ambroisie AM 192
With Telemann's Water Music

The Early Music ensemble Zefiro isn't exactly a household name. What's more, there are plenty of excellent versions of the *Water Music Suites* by better-known ensembles (take the brilliant recordings from the Academy of Ancient Music, for example). So why pick this one? Quite simply, when you listen to its performance, it really does feel as if Zefiro understands and encapsulates Handel's musical ideas. The ensemble performs on period instruments, which brings an added authenticity to its playing – and if you buy the whole album, you'll also get a brilliant recording of some less-well-known Baroque music by Telemann.

About Classic FM

If this series of books has whetted your appetite to find out more, one of the best ways to discover what you like about classical music is to listen to Classic FM. We broadcast a huge breadth of classical music 24 hours a day across the UK on 100–102 FM, on DAB digital radio, online at ClassicFM.com, on Sky Channel 0106, on Virgin Media channel 922 and on FreeSat channel 721. You can also download the free Classic FM App, which will enable you to listen to Classic FM on your iPhone, iPod, iPad, Blackberry or Android device.

As well as being able to listen online, you will find a host of interactive features about classical music, composers and musicians on our website, ClassicFM.com. When we first turned on Classic FM's transmitters more than two decades ago, we changed the face of classical music radio in the UK for ever. Now, we are doing the same online.

The very best way to find out more about which pieces of classical music you like is by going out and hearing a live performance by one of our great British orchestras for yourself. There is simply no substitute for seeing the whites of the eyes of a talented soloist as he or she performs a masterpiece on stage only a few feet in front of you, alongside a range of hugely accomplished musicians playing together as one.

Classic FM has a series of partnerships with orchestras across the country: the Bournemouth Symphony Orchestra, the London Symphony Orchestra, the Orchestra of Opera North, the Philharmonia Orchestra, the Royal Liverpool Philharmonic Orchestra, the Royal Northern Sinfonia and the Royal Scottish National Orchestra. And don't forget the brilliant young musicians of the National Children's Orchestra of Great Britain and of the National Youth Orchestra of Great Britain. To see if any of these orchestras have a concert coming up near you, log onto our website at ClassicFM.com and click on the 'Concerts and

Events' section. It will also include many other classical concerts – both professional and amateur – that are taking place near where you live.

Happy listening!

About the Author

Sam Jackson is the managing editor of Classic FM, responsible for all of the station's on-air programming and music output, a role he has held since 2011. Before then, he spent four years as the executive producer in charge of Classic FM's music programming. In his ten years at Classic FM, his programmes have been honoured by the Radio Academy Awards, the Arqiva Commercial Radio Awards and the New York International Radio Festival. He was chosen as one of the Radio Academy's '30 Under 30' for two consecutive years and, in 2012, he was the only person working in radio to be included in *Music Week*'s '30 Under 30'. In 2013, the Hospital Club named him as one of 'the 100 most influential, innovative and interesting individuals in the media and creative industries'. A proficient pianist and clarinettist, Sam holds a first-class degree in Music from the University of York. He sits on the governing body of Trinity Laban Conservatoire of Music and Dance and on the University of York Music Department's advisory board, as well as being a trustee of the Radio Academy. Previously, he enjoyed a career in front of the microphone, as a presenter on the children's digital radio station, Fun Kids. The author of two *Sunday Times* best-selling books about classical music, his new book about bringing up young children, *Diary of a Desperate Dad*, is published by Elliott & Thompson and he blogs regularly online about family life at diaryofadesperatedad.com

Index

Classical Recordings

Index

Classical Recordings

Index